ANIMAL TRACKS AND SIGNS

Gait Patterns

Walking

When an animal is walking, it lifts only one foot at a time. The stride (the distance between two tracks made by the same foot) will be small. The hind tracks will be close to the front tracks, perhaps even on top of them. In some animals, you may see marks of the body and tail dragging on the ground when the animal is moving slowly.

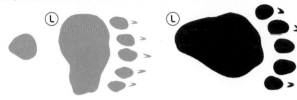

Bear tracks

Trotting

When an animal trots, it usually moves the front leg on one side at the same time as the hind leg on the other side – that is, the right front and left hind, and then the left front and right hind. The stride length is longer – there is a greater distance between tracks – and when an animal is trotting quickly, tracks may appear almost in a straight line.

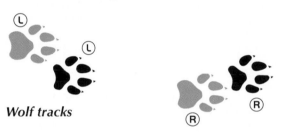

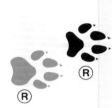

Wolf tracks

Galloping

A galloping or fast-running animal takes all four feet off the ground at one stage of the movement. The gait pattern shows groups of four tracks, with those of the hind feet appearing in front of those of the front feet. The animal takes off from its front feet and brings its hind legs up and forwards, landing on the hind legs first.

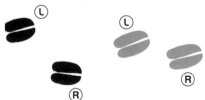

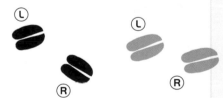

Deer tracks

Bounding/hopping

Like galloping animals, hopping animals have all four feet off the ground for a short period of the movement. Hopping animals, such as rabbits and hares, push off from the ground with the hind legs and then land with the hind feet slightly ahead of the front feet. You will see groups of four tracks, hind feet before the front.

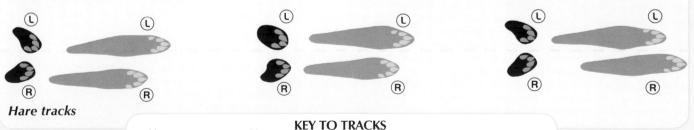

Hare tracks

KEY TO TRACKS
 Front foot   *Hind foot*   (R) *Right foot*   (L) *Left foot*

How to Track

Tracking an animal involves more than just finding a series of footprints on the ground. Tracks are one kind of evidence of an animal's presence, and an important one, but there are many other signs of activity to look for.

▲ *A Coyote feeds on the carcass of a Red Deer.*

Finding tracks

You are more likely to find tracks on soft surfaces. An animal's footprints rarely show on hard surfaces, such as rock, just as your footprints do not leave a mark on the pavement. Probably the easiest time to spot tracks is after a fall of snow. But remember that a print in snow appears much larger than the animal's actual foot. Otherwise, damp ground such as riverbanks, muddy paths, and sand are good places to look, particularly after rain. Tracks of the same animal will look different on different surfaces.

Droppings

After footprints, droppings, or scats, are one of the most obvious animal signs. They show that an animal is in the area, perhaps marking its territory, and can tell us something about what it eats. Some birds also produce pellets (*see* pages 142–143), which are the indigestible parts of a bird's food, such as insect wings and fur. These reveal a great deal about the eating habits of the bird.

Feeding signs

You can find the evidence of animals' feeding habits all around you. Look for areas of cropped grass and stripped leaves or bark. The position of a feeding sign on a tree is a clue to the animal that made it (*see* pages 60–61). You may also find a carcass – the remains of a dead animal – although these are generally swiftly dealt with by scavengers and insects.

Nests and homes

Many people have seen molehills and entrance holes to rabbit warrens and there are lots of other signs of homes to look for. You may spy a bird's nest in a hedge or high in a tree, but if you do, never disturb it, or any other animal home. Or you may see an area of flattened grass and plants where an animal has been sleeping. A tree hole might be home to a bird or a squirrel.

▲ *Blue Herons make their large nests high up in trees.*

Smaller creatures

It is not only large animals that leave signs of their activities. In any garden or park you can see the shimmering trails left by snails, leaves chewed by caterpillars, spiders' webs, and earthworm casts (excreted soil). Get into the habit of looking closely at plants for signs of these miniature worlds.

▲ *In winter, Red Deer eat woody growth and produce firm scats, like these; in summer, deer eat plants and the scats are softer.*

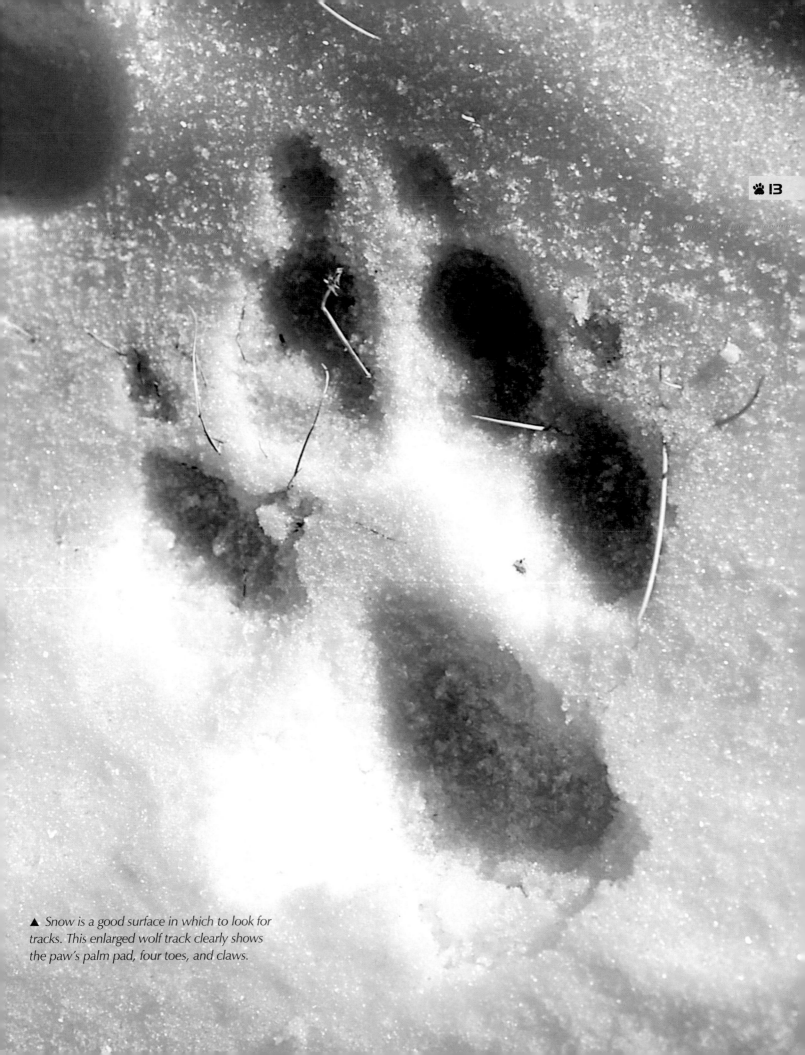

▲ *Snow is a good surface in which to look for tracks. This enlarged wolf track clearly shows the paw's palm pad, four toes, and claws.*

Recording Tracks

When you go out tracking, always take a notebook and ruler with you so you can write down the measurements of tracks you find and make notes on other signs, such as marks on a tree or changes in a nest or burrow. When you find animal tracks, you will want to record what they look like, too, to identify them later or add to your collection. The best ways of doing this are by making a sketch of the track, photographing it, or making a plaster cast.

Sketching

Making a drawing of the track is simple and requires the least equipment. Make sure you measure the track carefully and note every detail. Drawing on graph paper is the easiest way to get everything in proportion.

▲ *When photographing a track, always make sure you put an object next to it to show scale, such as a coin or a camera lens cover, as shown here next to a wolf track.*

Measuring Tracks

Keep a record of the tracks you find, noting all the details. Measure the total length and width of a track. Also measure the distance between individual tracks and groups of tracks as shown.

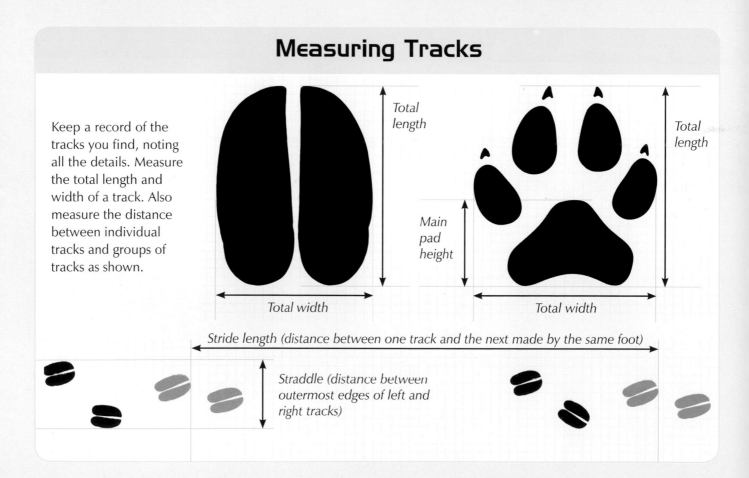

Total length

Total length

Main pad height

Total width

Total width

Stride length (distance between one track and the next made by the same foot)

Straddle (distance between outermost edges of left and right tracks)

Making Casts of Tracks

Making casts is a great way to record and collect your favourite animal tracks. You'll need to have some basic equipment with you and follow the simple steps below. The best casts are often made from tracks found in mud or fresh snow.

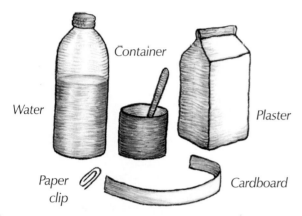

Water **Container** **Plaster** **Paper clip** **Cardboard**

❶ You will need water, plaster of Paris, a mixing container, thin cardboard, paper clips, and a ruler. Also take a clean bag to wrap the cast in.

❷ Use a strip of cardboard about 2 cm (1 in) wide to make a frame around your track. Push the card into the earth or snow and fix it with a paper clip or two.

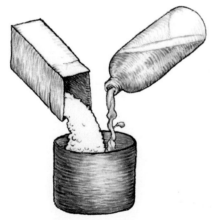

❸ Put some water in your container, add plaster of Paris, and mix. Add enough plaster to make a soft mixture about as thick as porridge.

❹ Pour the mixture into the frame to a depth of about 2 cm (1 in). Use the ruler to smooth the plaster into a flat surface. Leave the mixture to set for half an hour.

❺ Remove the frame, lift the cast carefully, wrap it, and take it home. Leave it to dry for a day. Clean it and, if you wish, paint it. Use a soft pencil to record on the bottom of the cast what animal made the track and when and where you made the cast.

Dingo

SIZE Body: 1 m (3¼ ft); tail: 36 cm (14 in)
RANGE Australia
HABITAT Forests, mountainous regions, plains, and deserts
FOOD Rabbits, other small mammals; working in packs, Dingoes also hunt larger prey such as kangaroos; also, when food is scarce, reptiles and insects
TRACKS AND SIGNS Tracks of the front feet are about 6 cm (2½ in) long, larger than those of the hind feet. There are clear claw marks. If you find the remains of prey, such as feathers and bones, outside a hole, you could be next to the entrance to a Dingo den.
COMMENTS Dingoes are descended from domesticated dogs introduced into Australia thousands of years ago.

▲ Wolves have great stamina and can cover many miles at a steady trot of 10 km/h (6 mph). During a chase, they can reach speeds of up to about 50 km/h (30 mph).

Tall Tails

A wolf pack is always led by a male and female pair, which are mates. They both carry their tails high to show their position. Other wolves must not carry their tails as high as the leaders, and low-ranking animals must keep their tails well down.

A tail held straight out shows a wolf is about to attack or hunt, while a drooping tail shows it is relaxed. When two wolves meet, they sniff each other to find out which one is dominant. The dominant wolf then raises his tail, while the other keeps his between his legs.

A high tail signifies a dominant wolf, a pack leader.

A horizontal or stiff tail tells us that this wolf is about to attack or hunt.

A drooping tail shows that this wolf is relaxed.

A tucked-in tail is a sign of a wolf's submission.

Otters

Otters, like weasels and skunks, belong to the mustelid family of flesh-eating mammals. They are expert swimmers and catch nearly all their food in water. While swimming they can close off their nostrils and ears. An otter's fur is short and very thick. It keeps the skin dry by trapping a layer of air around the body. Otters are very playful and inquisitive.

◄ *Otter droppings, like these from a Eurasian Otter, contain fish scales and bones from fish, frogs, and small mammals.*

Eurasian Otter

SIZE Body: 90 cm (35 in); tail: 40 cm (16 in)
RANGE Europe, Asia, northern Africa
HABITAT Rivers, lakes, estuaries
FOOD Mainly fish, shellfish, frogs, birds; also rodents
TRACKS AND SIGNS The Eurasian Otter spends much of its time in the water, but when on land it leaves tracks up to 7 cm (3 in) in length that often show all five toes and claw marks. Otters tend to bound along, leaving widely spaced groups of footprints. Look for remains of fish and shellfish shells on riverbanks. Also look for piles of droppings, which are often left on stones or logs on the riverbank, where they advertise the animal's presence to others.
COMMENTS Otters usually dig burrows in the riverbank. Outside the burrow you may see bare spots on the ground where the otters roll and marks left when they slide down through mud or snow to the water.

Cape Clawless Otter

SIZE Body: 95 cm (3 ft); tail: 65 cm (26 in)
RANGE Africa south of the Sahara, except rainforests
HABITAT Streams, lakes, rocky coasts
FOOD Shellfish such as crabs; molluscs, including octopus, and frogs; also eats fish and worms
TRACKS AND SIGNS Its 10-cm (4-in) prints on muddy shores show five long toes on each foot. Close to the water, look for piles of droppings, which usually contain the remains of crabs.
COMMENTS The Clawless Otter has no claws. Its sensitive feet are just right for finding shellfish in muddy river bottoms and holding them as it feeds.

Giant Otter

SIZE Body: 1.8 m (6 ft); tail: 65 cm (26 in)
RANGE Northern South America to Paraguay and northern Argentina
HABITAT Rivers and lakes in tropical rainforests
FOOD Fish is the main food, but also eats crabs, snakes, and even small caiman
TRACKS AND SIGNS This otter's large feet have thick webbing between each toe. Its tracks are similar to those of the Eurasian Otter but three to four times larger. Look for areas of riverbank cleared of plants, where Giant Otters like to lie and groom themselves.
COMMENTS The largest otter by length and the largest of the mustelid group of animals, this otter is now endangered. It is much noisier than other otters and makes loud screaming calls.

▲ *This Sea Otter is floating on its back while it eats a meal of abalone, a type of shellfish.*

Signs of the Sea Otter

Sea Otters live in the ocean and spend much more time in water than other otters do, so it is rare to find their tracks on land. But if you are in the area where Sea Otters live – the rocky Pacific coastline of North America – you may be lucky enough to spot these wonderful creatures bobbing up and down in the waves. Look for their shiny black, whiskery noses among beds of seaweed floating on the water surface. And you might spot a Sea Otter feeding. The animal lies on its back with a rock on its chest, banging a clam or other shellfish against the rock until its hard shell is broken, before eating the soft flesh inside. Like other otters, Sea Otters are very playful and can be seen leaping and surfing in the waves.

▲ *This Common Raccoon has just rummaged through a dustbin for scraps, leaving its characteristic mess behind.*

South American Coati

SIZE Body: 65 cm (26 in); tail: 70 cm (28 in)
RANGE Tropical South America
HABITAT Forest and woodland
FOOD Fruit, small mammals, and other creatures such as spiders, centipedes, and insects
TRACKS AND SIGNS Also known as the Brown-nosed Coati, this animal has feet smaller than those of the raccoon, with shorter toes. Its hind tracks are about 4.5 cm (1¾ in) wide, and its prints usually show all five toes and claws. These animals are active during the day and are far from shy, so they are quite easy to spot. They climb trees to feed on fruit but spend most of their time on the ground.
COMMENTS Like raccoons, coati will look through dustbins for food.

Ⓗ

Happy Eaters

One of the secrets of the Common Raccoon's success is its willingness to eat lots of different kinds of food. Animals that are not fussy are less likely to have trouble finding something to eat. The raccoon has very nimble fingers, able to pick leaves and berries as well as dig out juicy bits from shellfish. It is also skilled at finding its way into dustbins and outbuildings to feed on scraps and can even untie ropes and open jars.

A raccoon sorting through rubbish is now a common night-time sight in many towns and cities in North America. Many people want to scare raccoons away from their garden, but if you want to attract these animals in order to watch them, try putting out some of their favourite foods. These include peanuts, bread, and cat and dog food. Do not put food out too regularly, though, or the raccoons will become dependent on your supplies. And never go too close or try to feed raccoons by hand – they may bite!

Mongooses and Civets

Mongooses and civets are small carnivores. There are about 37 different types of mongoose, which all live in Africa and Asia. These ground-living animals have a long, slim body. Civets also have a long, slim body and tail, but most have cat-like striped or spotted markings. Most civets are active at night and are good climbers.

▶ *A group of Meerkats is called a "mob" or a "gang". If a mob becomes too large, it may split into smaller mobs.*

White-tailed Mongoose

SIZE Body: 70 cm (28 in); tail: 48 cm (19 in)
RANGE Africa south of the Sahara (except the forests of west, southwest, or central Africa); southwest Arabia
HABITAT Savanna and grassland
FOOD Insects, snakes, other small animals, birds' eggs, fruit
TRACKS AND SIGNS The White-tailed Mongoose has five toes on each foot, but only four show in its tracks, which are about 4.5 cm (1¾ in) long. Strong claw marks can usually be seen, too, with the marks of the left and right claws appearing well behind the claw marks of the central toes.
COMMENTS This large mongoose does not live in big groups like the Meerkat does, and it generally moves alone or in pairs. It is usually active at night.

Meerkat or Suricate

SIZE Body: 35 cm (14 in); tail: 25 cm (10 in)
RANGE Southern Africa
HABITAT Dry open country
FOOD Insects and other small animals, eggs, plants
TRACKS AND SIGNS This mongoose has four toes on each foot, all of which show in its tracks, which measure about 3 cm (1¼ in) in length. Its claws, too, show clearly in the tracks. Those on the front feet are longer than those on the back. Look for holes around the tracks, which show where the animals have been digging for insects.
COMMENTS Meerkats live in large family groups of up to 30 animals, so you are likely to find lots of tracks in the same place. They are usually active during the day. Look for their underground burrows, which may have several different entrances.

African Civet

SIZE Body: 90 cm (35 in); tail: 45 cm (18 in)

RANGE Africa from south of the Sahara to northern and eastern South Africa

HABITAT Forest and savanna

FOOD Rodents and other small animals, reptiles, insects, fruit, plants; also eats carrion

TRACKS AND SIGNS Has five toes on its front and hind feet but only four show in the tracks. Short claw marks also appear. Tracks are around 6 cm (2¼ in) long and look similar to dog tracks, but check for the small dip at the back edge of main pads. Look near tracks for dropping sites (latrines), which may be used by several animals. Scats contain plant matter, hairs, feathers, and insect remains.

COMMENTS The African Civet secretes a smelly black fluid from a gland near its tail and uses it to mark rocks and trees in its home range.

Feeding Signs

Meerkats quite quickly get used to humans and can be wonderful to watch as they go about their daily routine. They live in very well-organized groups, which usually contain two or three families. These families share the duties of caring for the young and keeping guard. While most of the group feeds, one Meerkat acts as sentry, often sitting up on its hind legs for a better view. If it spots a predator, it barks loudly so the rest of the group can dive for cover or hide in their burrow. Other animals act as babysitters, keeping an eye on young while their parents are off searching for food.

▼ *These Meerkats are warming up in the early morning sun after a cold desert night. They absorb heat through their sparsely furred underside while standing on their hind legs.*

Ⓗ

Western Gorilla

◀ SCALE: ¹/₇ *life-size*

SIZE Body: 1.9 m (6¼ ft); tail: none
RANGE Central and East Africa
HABITAT Tropical rainforests of
Central Africa; (Mountain Gorillas
live in cloud forests on the Virunga
Volcanoes, East Africa)
FOOD Mainly leaves, shoots, stems, and
some fruits, flowers, and insects
TRACKS AND SIGNS The footprint is up to
about 28 cm (11 in) long, and the big toe
stands away from the side of the foot like
a thumb. Only the knuckles of the hands
show in the front tracks. Gorillas make
many loud calls to keep in touch with
others in the troop, so you may hear them
even if you cannot see them.
COMMENTS Gorillas are active during the
day and sleep in tree nests at night,
which they make fresh every day.
They usually move only two or three
kilometres a day as they feed.

▲ *Chimpanzee scats often contain fruit seeds, which
become scattered around the forest to grow into new plants.*

Handprints

The prints shown for the primates on these pages
are all hind tracks. Gorillas and chimpanzees do
not make full handprints, only little rounded marks
made as they lean on their knuckles. Try making
your own knuckle prints on a soft surface such as
damp sand to see what these look like.

Gibbons and Orangutans

Orangutans are great apes, like chimpanzees and gorillas. They are tree dwellers and rarely walk on the ground. Gibbons, also called the lesser apes, are well adapted for life in the trees, climbing and swinging from branch to branch very skilfully. Gibbons and orangutans live in Asia, and their tracks are very rare.

▶ *A gibbon's wrists have flexible ball-and-socket joints, which help it to swing smoothly from branch to branch.*

Orangutan

SIZE Body: 1.5 m (5 ft); tail: none
RANGE Borneo and Sumatra
HABITAT Tropical rainforest
FOOD Mainly fruit; also leaves, insects, perhaps small animals and birds' eggs
TRACKS AND SIGNS There are two species of orangutan, the Bornean and Sumatran. Both are extremely rare, so you would be very lucky to see one. But just in case, look very carefully at trees that are fruiting, particularly those such as durian, which orangutans love. Check for signs of tree nests made by the apes, large branches moving, and piles of fruit skins under trees. And listen for the males' loud roaring call.
COMMENTS Like chimpanzees, the orangutan has been spotted using tools in the wild. It drapes large leaves over itself for shelter from the sun or rain and uses sticks to scratch itself or to extract insects from nests. It also uses sticks to help it reach fruit at the end of branches.

Black Gibbon

SIZE Body: 65 cm (26 in); tail: none
RANGE Southeastern China, parts of Laos and Vietnam
HABITAT Tropical rainforest
FOOD Mainly fruit; also eats leaves, insects, and other small creatures
TRACKS AND SIGNS You are much more likely to hear gibbons than see them, as most of their activity takes place in the treetops high above your head. But they do make a wide range of loud calls to keep in touch with each other, warn of danger, and defend their territory. Some of these calls can be heard several kilometres away. Males and females may sing "duets" together.
COMMENTS Gibbons don't make nests but just sleep while sitting up in the trees.

Swinging Gibbons

Gibbons are the most acrobatic of all tree-living animals and travel through the trees at amazing speed. They swing from branch to branch on their long arms in a form of movement called brachiation. A gibbon rarely uses its feet for grasping but often swings its legs forwards to help propel it to the next handhold. Sometimes the gibbon will even let go both hands and just leap through the air to the next tree.

▼ *Like gorillas, orangutans make a new nest from branches and leaves each evening. This Sumatran Orangutan has made her nest in a tree and is sitting in it with her young.*

Hoolock Gibbon

SIZE Body: 65 cm (26 in); tail: none
RANGE India, Bangladesh, Burma
HABITAT Tropical rainforest
FOOD Mainly fruit; also eats leaves, insects, and other small creatures
TRACKS AND SIGNS Tracks are almost never seen, as this animal rarely comes down to the ground. Listen for this gibbon's very loud screeching calls.
COMMENTS Gibbons live in family groups of a male, a female, and their young.

◄ LIFE-SIZE
*footprint of
Indian Rhino*

Indian Rhinoceros

◄ SCALE: ¹/₁₀ *life-size*

SIZE Body: 3.8 m (12½ ft);
tail: 80 cm (32 in)
RANGE Small area of northeastern
India; once more widespread
HABITAT Grassland, floodplains,
wooded meadows
FOOD Grass, aquatic plants, other plants
TRACKS AND SIGNS The tracks are similar to those
of the White Rhino but with no indent at the back
edge. Signs that rhinos are close by include large piles
of droppings, called middens, near mud wallows and
paths. There may be horn marks gouged into the
ground around the piles. Male rhinos also spray urine
around to mark their territory.
COMMENTS Rhinos love to wallow in muddy water
to cool themselves down and escape biting flies. Look
for hollows in the mud made by the rhino's huge
body. There may also be marks where the animal has
rubbed its muddy body against a tree.

Brazilian Tapir

◄ SCALE: ¹/₁₀ *life-size*

SIZE Body: 2 m (6½ ft);
tail: 1 m (3¼ ft)
RANGE South America: Venezuela
to Argentina
HABITAT Rainforest and woodland, always
near water
FOOD Aquatic plants, fruit, stems of land plants
TRACKS AND SIGNS Look for the paths worn down
by tapirs on their way to water, as they quickly
flatten any vegetation. This animal is often on
muddy ground, so its distinctive three-toed tracks,
which are up to 18 cm (7 in) long, are frequently
seen, but the creature itself is more difficult to spot.
COMMENTS Tapirs are good swimmers. If they
become frightened, they will plunge into water to
escape if they can.

◄ LIFE-SIZE *footprint of
Brazilian Tapir*

Hippos

There are only two species of hippopotamus, both of which live in Africa. The full-sized Hippo moves easily in water and can even walk along the river bottom. Its nostrils close off so it does not get water in its nose. It spends its days resting in the water and comes out at night to feed on land. The Pygmy Hippo also feeds at night. Hippos have almost hairless skin, which dries out if not regularly submerged. Although they are plant eaters, they can be very dangerous. Track a hippo only with an experienced guide.

◀ LIFE-SIZE
Hippo track

Pygmy Hippopotamus

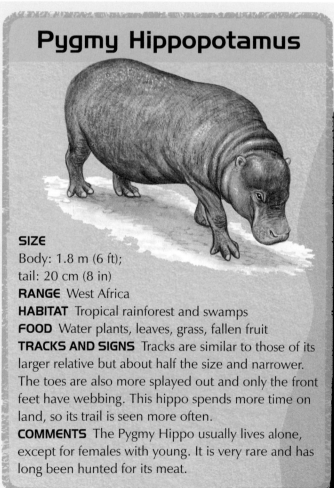

SIZE
Body: 1.8 m (6 ft);
tail: 20 cm (8 in)
RANGE West Africa
HABITAT Tropical rainforest and swamps
FOOD Water plants, leaves, grass, fallen fruit
TRACKS AND SIGNS Tracks are similar to those of its larger relative but about half the size and narrower. The toes are also more splayed out and only the front feet have webbing. This hippo spends more time on land, so its trail is seen more often.
COMMENTS The Pygmy Hippo usually lives alone, except for females with young. It is very rare and has long been hunted for its meat.

◄ *A dominant male marks his territory by wagging his tail to scatter his dung around. The scattered dung acts as a warning to other males that they should act submissively or expect a fight. Groups of female Hippos live with their young in the territory of a dominant male.*

Yawning Hippos

A Hippo can open its huge mouth amazingly wide, revealing large teeth protruding as much as 30 cm (12 in) above the gum. But if you do see a Hippo yawn, beware. It isn't tired – this is actually a threat display, and Hippos have been known to charge when disturbed.

Hippopotamus

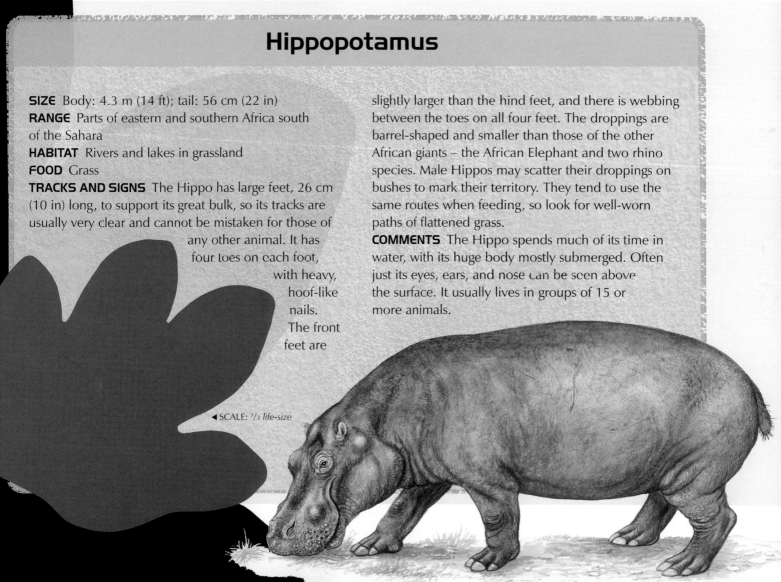

SIZE Body: 4.3 m (14 ft); tail: 56 cm (22 in)
RANGE Parts of eastern and southern Africa south of the Sahara
HABITAT Rivers and lakes in grassland
FOOD Grass
TRACKS AND SIGNS The Hippo has large feet, 26 cm (10 in) long, to support its great bulk, so its tracks are usually very clear and cannot be mistaken for those of any other animal. It has four toes on each foot, with heavy, hoof-like nails. The front feet are slightly larger than the hind feet, and there is webbing between the toes on all four feet. The droppings are barrel-shaped and smaller than those of the other African giants – the African Elephant and two rhino species. Male Hippos may scatter their droppings on bushes to mark their territory. They tend to use the same routes when feeding, so look for well-worn paths of flattened grass.
COMMENTS The Hippo spends much of its time in water, with its huge body mostly submerged. Often just its eyes, ears, and nose can be seen above the surface. It usually lives in groups of 15 or more animals.

◄ SCALE: ¹/₃ life-size

▲ *A Springbok leaps high into the air. The height it reaches shows any potential predator that this is no easy catch.*

Impala

SIZE Body: 1.5 m
(5 ft); tail: 40 cm (16 in)
RANGE Eastern Africa: Kenya
to northern South Africa
HABITAT Open woodland and
grassland, usually near water
FOOD Grass and leaves
TRACKS AND SIGNS The tracks of this antelope are
5 cm (2 in) long and show pointed toe prints, or
cleaves. The front and hind feet are about the same
size. Prints may be slightly blurred by tufts of hair on
the feet. Trails are often seen to and from water holes.
The male leaves piles of droppings in special places in
his territory during the mating season to alert females
to his presence.
COMMENTS Impala usually live in large
herds, led by dominant male
animals. Males mark their
territorial boundaries with urine
and droppings. Impala are fast
runners and can leap into the
air as they run.

The Springing Springbok

The Springbok gets its name from its habit of
making a series of bounds into the air, leaping as
high as 3.5 m (11½ ft). It holds its legs stiff and
straight as it bounds. The movement is called
"stotting" or "pronking" and may help to warn
others in the herd that predators are near. It may
also send a message to the predator that this is a
speedy, agile animal and the hunter should look
elsewhere for a meal.

Camels

▲ *In many parts of North Africa, camel trains such as this one in Somalia are still a very important form of transport.*

There are just four species in the camel family: the Bactrian (two-humped) Camel, the Dromedary (one-humped) Camel, and the Guanaco and Vicuña, both of which live in South America. Llamas and Alpacas are domestic animals, bred from the Guanaco for their thick wool. All these animals are plant eaters and can eat tough, even spiny, plants. A camel's humps are not for storing water, as people once thought, but for storing fat. This provides the camel with food when supplies are scarce in its desert home.

Bactrian Camel

SIZE Body: 3.5 m (11½ ft); tail: 50 cm (20 in)
RANGE Gobi Desert, Central Asia
HABITAT Desert and steppe
FOOD Grass, leaves, almost any plant
TRACKS AND SIGNS The Bactrian, like its relatives, has only two toes on each foot. The foot bones are expanded sideways as support for the broad flat pads on each foot, and there are nails on the upper surface of the toes. This foot structure stops the camel from sinking too deeply when it walks on soft, sandy soil, leaving tracks about 23 cm (9 in) wide.
COMMENTS The Bactrian has very long shaggy hair to keep it warm in the cold Gobi winter. In summer the hair is shed in large patches, leaving the animal's skin almost bare.

◄ SCALE: ¹/₆ life-size

Dromedary Camel

SIZE Body: 3.5 m (11½ ft); tail: 50 cm (20 in)
RANGE North Africa, Middle East; introduced in Australia
HABITAT Dry grassland, desert, plains
FOOD Plants, including tough, thorny bushes
TRACKS AND SIGNS Like the Bactrian, the Dromedary leaves splayed tracks up to 23 cm (9 in) wide and has feet adapted for walking on sand.
COMMENTS Dromedaries are now extinct in the wild, except in Australia, where there is a large feral (semi-wild) population. Domesticated camels are used as beasts of burden and for camel racing.

◄ SCALE: ¹/₆ life-size

▲ *A camel's feet are well adapted to walking on sand. They widen at the bottom, spreading the animal's weight over a large area, which prevents it from sinking.*

Desert Dweller

The Dromedary Camel is very well adapted to desert life. When going without food for long periods, it gets nutrients from fat reserves in its hump. When going without water, it can lose more than a quarter of its body weight yet remain healthy. When it finds water, it can drink up to 100 litres (22 gallons) in ten minutes to replace what it has lost. Its thick eyelashes protect its eyes from sand, and its small, narrow nostrils can close to keep out dust. Its body temperature drops at night and rises during the day, so it does not often need to sweat to cool itself – sweating uses water.

◀ LIFE-SIZE *footprint of Dromedary or Bactrian camel*

Vicuña

SIZE Body: 1.8 m (6 ft); tail: 25 cm (10 in)
RANGE Western South America: Peru and Chile
HABITAT High grassland
FOOD Grass and small plants
TRACKS AND SIGNS Like its relatives, the Vicuña has two toes on each foot, but its feet are smaller and narrower than those of camels. Listen for its alarm call, which is a clear whistling sound. Look for droppings, too. Vicuñas live in groups and usually leave their droppings in communal heaps to mark their territory.
COMMENTS The Vicuña has very fine but dense fur and often rolls in the dust to clean and scratch itself. You may see signs of this rolling activity on the ground.

A Beaver Lodge

When a family of beavers moves into an area, it makes far-reaching changes. The family begins by damming a stream, using branches, tree trunks, and mud to create a quiet area of water where they can build their lodge. The dam also makes a storage area for winter food. The beavers cut extra branches in autumn and store them under water near the dam. The lodge, too, is built from branches and plastered with mud. The entrance is below the water surface well away from predators. The beaver's work is never finished. It constantly has to repair the dam and lodge, adding more mud, twigs, and sticks.

▼ A North American Beaver busies itself with repairs to a dam. The important work of maintaining the dam is shared by the whole family group.

Paca

SIZE Body: 75 cm (30 in); tail: 3 cm (1¼ in)
RANGE Southern Mexico to northern Argentina
HABITAT Forest near water
FOOD Leaves, roots, seeds; also eats fallen fruits such as avocados
TRACKS AND SIGNS Another large stocky rodent, the Paca often leaves well-used trails and clear tracks on muddy river banks. It has four toes on the front feet and five on the hind. The hind tracks are usually slightly larger than the front tracks, which are about 4.5 cm (1¾ in) wide. Other signs of the Paca are burrows in the river bank or among tree roots. Each burrow may have several exits just in case.
COMMENTS Pacas are good swimmers and often run for the water when in danger. They are usually active at night. They may bury seeds when food is plentiful and dig them up when they need them.

Rats and Mice

Rats and mice are some of the world's most successful mammals, and hundreds of species live in many different habitats. The secret of their success is their adaptability – they eat almost anything and can live almost anywhere. Some rats and mice generally live near humans, where they know they will always have food supplies. Rats and mice are also important prey animals for many other kinds of creatures.

◀ *A Brown Rat feeds in the undergrowth. It comes out to forage at night and will eat almost anything.*

Brown Rat

SIZE Body: 28 cm (11 in); tail: 23 cm (9 in)
RANGE Originally Asia but now worldwide

HABITAT Everywhere, usually near humans
FOOD Seeds, fruits, leaves; also small animals, scraps
TRACKS AND SIGNS The Brown Rat has four toes on the front feet and five on the hind feet, all of which usually show in its tracks. The front tracks are about 2.5 cm (1 in) wide. The hind feet are longer, measuring about 5 cm (2 in). As it bounds along, the Brown Rat leaves groups of four prints. Rats and mice often pass urine as they run, so look for streaks of urine near trails.
COMMENTS The Brown Rat is one of the most widespread and common animals of all. It is a burrower and may disturb foundations by digging under buildings.

Ⓗ

House Mouse

SIZE Body: up to 10 cm (4 in); tail: 10 cm (4 in)
RANGE Originally Asia but now worldwide
HABITAT Very varied, usually near humans
FOOD Seeds, grain, human foods
TRACKS AND SIGNS Tracks of this little creature are seen only in soft surfaces, such as snow or mud. Where they do appear, tracks are under 15 mm (½ in) long, and show four toes on front feet and five on back feet. The tail may appear in trails in snow. Look for small round droppings near tracks and feeding places.
COMMENTS Like the Brown Rat, the House Mouse is extremely common and can do great damage to stored food, being able to chew through tough bags and packaging.

Ⓗ

Deer Mouse

SIZE Body: up to 10 cm (4 in); tail: 10 cm (4 in)
RANGE North America
HABITAT Forest, grassland, scrub
FOOD Seeds, nuts, berries, fruit; also insects, other small creatures, carrion
TRACKS AND SIGNS These little mice are generally active at night so you are not likely to spot them, but you may see their tracks on soft surfaces, such as mud or snow. Its tracks are very like those of the House Mouse, but these mice are less likely to be around human homes. The tail may show in trails in the snow.
COMMENTS Deer Mice are extremely common and will live in almost any kind of habitat with sufficient food. They may find their way into sheds or other buildings for protection during winter.

Food Pests

Like all rodents, rats and mice have sharp teeth and can chew their way through wood and wire, as well as cloth bags and other storage materials. They can also climb well and jump. Once they get access to stores, rats and mice not only eat the food but also spoil vast amounts with their droppings and urine. They carry a number of serious diseases, such as rabies, so it is not safe to eat food that rats and mice have spoiled. With a plentiful food supply, rats and mice reproduce rapidly, hugely increasing the amount of damage they can wreak. Females can bear several litters of 20 or more young in a single year.

▼ *Rats can destroy grain supplies and will reproduce very quickly, so that within a few weeks there may be thousands of them feasting on the stores.*

Fungi

Many animals feed on fungi, particularly in autumn. Some fungi are large, and an animal may eat part of it and leave the rest. Look for the large tooth marks of squirrels and small teeth marks of voles and mice. Some birds peck at fungi in search of fungus grubs, leaving holes made by their beak.

◄ *Tooth marks on the top of this mushroom cap show where it has been gnawed at by a small rodent.*

Identifying the Signs

The remains of the cones and hazelnuts below have been left by either squirrels or wood mice. Can you tell which is which?

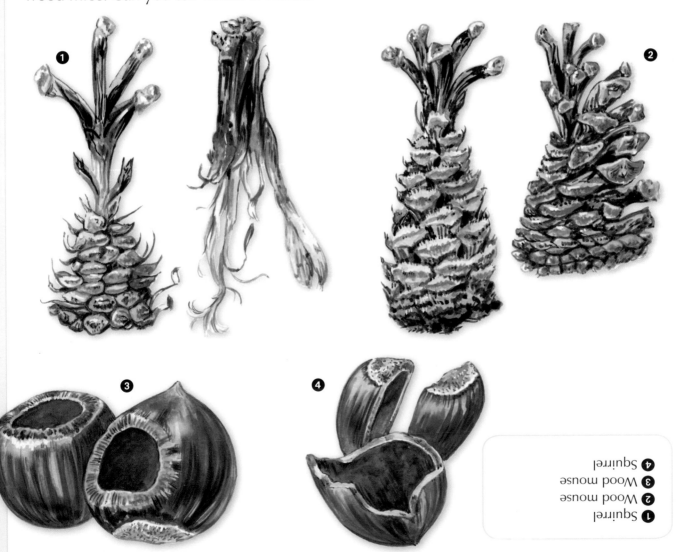

1 Squirrel
2 Wood mouse
3 Wood mouse
4 Squirrel

Porcupines

Porcupines are large rodents with long, sharp, loosely attached spines, called quills, on their backs and tails. They live in Africa, Asia, and North and South America. African and Asian species live mostly on the ground. American species spend much of their time in trees and their feet have strong claws and pebbly soles to give a good grip. If threatened, porcupines raise their quills to make themselves look bigger and may rattle the quills and thrash their spiny tails around. Some species will also charge backwards to drive their quills into the enemy.

▲ *Porcupines make their dens in caves, hollow trees, or, as here, decaying logs. Droppings surround the entrance.*

North American Porcupine

SIZE Body: 80 cm (32 in); tail: 30 cm (12 in)

RANGE North America: Alaska to Mexico

HABITAT Tundra, forest, scrub

FOOD Leaves, roots, flowers, seeds, bark, conifer needles

TRACKS AND SIGNS This large rodent has sharp quills to protect it and so it rarely runs. There are four toes on the front feet, five on the hind feet, and the tracks are easy to recognize because they have long claw marks and the soles have a pebbly surface. The hind tracks are up to 11.5 cm (4½ in) long, the front up to 7.5 cm (3 in) long. The tracks point inwards and you may see marks of the tail dragging along.

COMMENTS Look for chewed bark and twigs under trees – often a sign of porcupine activity. You may also see piles of droppings under trees.

Crested Porcupine

SIZE Body: 80 cm (32 in); tail: 12.5 cm (5 in)

RANGE North and sub-Saharan East and Central Africa; introduced in Italy

HABITAT Varied: forest, grassland, rocky scrub

FOOD Bulbs, roots, fruit, bark; some insects

TRACKS AND SIGNS This is the largest African rodent, with prints up to 8 cm (3¼ in) long. The front and hind prints show four toes and claws – there are five toes on the front feet but the first is very small and doesn't always show on tracks. The tracks are sometimes mistaken for those of the Honey Badger (see pages 34–35), but the porcupine's claws are much shorter.

COMMENTS Look for quills, which may drop out as the animal moves around.

Tree Porcupine

SIZE Body: 60 cm (24 in); tail: 50 cm (20 in)
RANGE Northeast South America
HABITAT Tropical forest
FOOD Leaves, stems, fruit, bark
TRACKS AND SIGNS The Tree Porcupine's feet are specialized for climbing, with long curved claws on each toe. It can climb trees within a couple of days of being born and spends most of its life in trees, so you are very unlikely to see its tracks on the ground. One sign to listen for is the growling sounds it makes; it also sits and shakes its spines to warn off enemies.
COMMENTS This porcupine has a prehensile (gripping) tail to help it climb. There are no spines on the tail, and the upper part is bare of fur and has a rough pad to help the animal hold on tight.

Porcupine Quills

Porcupine quills are a type of hair with a thick covering, and there are about 30,000 on most porcupines. The quills are very sharp and have tiny backwards-facing barbs on the end. Once the quill is in the victim's skin, the barbs catch hold and make it very difficult to remove – but they come away from the porcupine easily. The more the victim struggles to get the quill out, the deeper in it goes, and the animal may die if the wound becomes infected.

▶ *Porcupines in some parts of the world destroy trees by eating their bark. This dead tree in India shows signs of having been feasted upon by porcupines.*

Koala

SIZE Body: 80 cm (32 in); tail: none
RANGE Eastern Australia
HABITAT Eucalyptus forest, woodland
FOOD Eucalyptus leaves and shoots
TRACKS AND SIGNS The Koala spends much of its time in trees, but its tracks are sometimes seen beneath its feeding trees. Its footprints are up to 15 cm (6 in) long, and on the front foot, the first and second toes point away from the rest of the foot. The large, curved claws also leave marks. Look for scratches in tree trunks left by the Koala as it climbs and for droppings under their feeding trees.

Koala droppings contain bits of leaf and may smell of eucalyptus.
COMMENTS The Koala's front feet are adapted for holding its food – the first toes can be held against the other three to help the animal grip.

Wombat Burrows

All three wombat species use their long claws to dig vast burrows in which to shelter during the day. The burrow may stretch many metres and be up to 2 m (6 ft) deep. The animal digs with its front feet and kicks the soil out of the way with its back feet. Any plant roots in the way are quickly disposed of by the wombat's strong teeth. The entrance is quite large to admit the bulky wombat and often oval in shape. A wombat may have three or more burrows, and several wombats may use the same burrow.

▶ *A Common Wombat young clings to its mother's back in a burrow. Wombats can be very aggressive if disturbed.*

Egg-laying Mammals

The echidnas and Platypus are the only animals in a group of mammals called monotremes. These animals all lay eggs instead of giving birth to live young. However, they do have body hair, and they feed their young on milk like other mammals do. Both the Long- and Short-nosed Echidnas are covered in coarse hairs and spines. The Platypus has a beak-like mouth and webbed feet and spends much of its life in water.

◀ *Short-nosed Echidnas may be found in many environments in Australia, including urban parkland.*

Long-nosed Echidna

SIZE Body: 80 cm (32 in); tail: 5 cm (2 in)
RANGE New Guinea
HABITAT Forest
FOOD Earthworms and other soil-living creatures
TRACKS AND SIGNS The tracks of these creatures are rare. It has five toes on each foot, and the three middle ones usually have sharp claws for digging. The male has a spur on each back leg.

COMMENTS Instead of teeth, this animal has small hooked spines on its tongue, which help it gather earthworms to eat.

Short-nosed Echidna

SIZE Body: 36 cm (14 in); tail: 10 cm (4 in)

RANGE Australia, Tasmania, New Guinea
HABITAT Grassland, forest, plains, rocky areas
FOOD Ants and termites
TRACKS AND SIGNS The front footprints, which turn slightly inwards, are 4 cm (1½ in) long and show all five toes and strong claws. The hind prints show four claws, two of them very long. These long claws help the echidna groom itself. Look out for damaged ant and termite nests and rotting logs that have been torn apart by echidnas searching for food.

COMMENTS Short-nosed Echidnas shelter in hollow logs, among rocks, or in burrows abandoned by other animals. They will dig themselves into the soil if in danger.

Platypus

SIZE Body: 40 cm (16 in); tail: 15 cm (6 in)
RANGE Eastern Australia, Tasmania
HABITAT Lakes and rivers in wooded areas
FOOD Shellfish, larvae, frogs, fish
TRACKS AND SIGNS The Platypus is a strong swimmer with webbed feet, but its tracks are sometimes seen on muddy river banks. When it walks on land, the webbing is folded back so its claw marks show in its tracks. The webbing on the hind feet, which are 5 cm (2 in) long, stops further back before the toes. The tail drags on the ground and shows in trails.
COMMENTS The male Platypus has a spur on each ankle that connects to poison glands in the thighs. The spurs are used against predators or rival males but not to kill prey.

Platypus Burrows

The Platypus digs short burrows in the riverbank above the water level for shelter. But in the breeding season, the female digs a longer burrow and lays her eggs in a chamber at the end, on a nest of dry grass and leaves. She stays with her eggs most of the time to keep them warm, leaving only briefly to feed. When the young hatch, they are tiny, blind, and helpless, and they stay in the burrow for several months. Look out for burrow entrances, which often show an area of flattened mud leading down to the water.

▼ *This Platypus is diving in search of freshwater crayfish, which it digs out of the river bed using its snout. It carries them to the surface in its cheek pouches.*

Frilled Lizard

SIZE Body: 30 cm (12 in);
tail: 60 cm (24 in)
RANGE Northern Australia, New Guinea
HABITAT Dry forest, grassy woodland
FOOD Ants, termites, other insects, spiders, small lizards and mammals
TRACKS AND SIGNS This lizard stays up in trees nearly all the time and lives in grassy areas, so tracks are rarely seen; you may spot it on low branches. In spring and summer you may find its open nest dug about 10 cm (4 in) into sandy soil, with a clutch of 8–15 soft-shelled small white eggs. The eggs are tiny – only about 1 cm (½ in) long.
COMMENTS If you get close to a Frilled Lizard, you may be lucky enough to see its startling display. If threatened, the lizard opens its mouth wide and hisses, unfurling a brightly coloured ruff of skin up to 30 cm (20 in) wide around its neck to make itself look bigger. It may then run away on its hind legs.

Speedy Climbers

Geckos can scamper up the smoothest walls and walk upside down on ceilings with the greatest ease. They can do this because of a little disc-like pad at the end of each toe. The pads on a single foot are covered in millions of tiny bristles tipped with suction cups, which help the feet hold fast to almost any surface.

▼ *The tuatara lives in colder climates than most reptiles. It is active at temperatures as low as 7°C (45°F), and those above 28°C (82°F) can kill it. It is active mainly at night.*

Tuatara

There are just two kinds of tuatara, both living on islands off New Zealand. The tuatara looks like a lizard but is actually in a group all of its own. It is like related reptiles that lived more than 130 million years ago. Tuataras shelter in burrows and feed on small creatures such as crickets, worms, snails, and lizards.

Turtles and Tortoises

There are about 230 different species of turtles and tortoises. Some live on land, others in fresh water, and a few very large turtles live in the sea. Most have a hard shell made of horn and bone to protect the soft body. The shell is in two parts, the upper shell (the carapace) and the lower (the plastron). Most turtles and tortoises can pull their head under the shell for protection. They have no teeth. Instead, they have hard beaks.

▲ *A hatchling Leatherback Turtle makes its way across the beach to the sea, leaving a trail of V-shaped tracks in the sand.*

Spur-thighed Tortoise

SIZE 15 cm (6 in) long
RANGE North Africa, southern Europe, Middle East
HABITAT Woodland, cultivated land, meadows
FOOD Mainly plants and some insects and other small creatures such as snails; also carnivore droppings to obtain calcium, which, like all tortoises and turtles, they need to keep their bones and shells in good condition
TRACKS AND SIGNS The tracks of this species show five very broad, rounded claws on the front feet and four on the hind feet. The tracks are about 3 cm (1¼ in) wide. Look for small, pointed droppings, too, which contain mainly plant matter.
COMMENTS If it feels threatened or scared, the Spur-thighed Tortoise, like most other tortoises, can pull its head and legs into its shell for protection.

Common Snapping Turtle

SIZE Shell: up to 50 cm (20 in); tail: up to 40 cm (15 in)
RANGE Eastern North America, Mexico, Central America
HABITAT Marshes, ponds, rivers, lakes
FOOD All kinds of water and bankside life, including fish, amphibians, mammals, birds, and plants
TRACKS AND SIGNS This turtle spends much of its time in water, but you may see its tracks, which are 5 cm (2 in) wide, on muddy banks. The long tail may leave a line between the footprints.
COMMENTS An excellent swimmer, the Common Snapping Turtle also likes to wait for its prey at the river bottom, hidden by aquatic plants. In the cooler areas of their range, Common Snapping Turtles hibernate in winter.

Leatherback Turtle

SIZE Up to 2 m (6½ ft)

RANGE Warm areas of all the world's oceans

HABITAT Deep open ocean

FOOD Mainly jellyfish

TRACKS AND SIGNS Males never leave the sea. The female does so only to nest, choosing a moonless night so that predators do not see her, and laying eggs several times a month from May to July. The nests are hidden beneath the sand above the high-tide line. After 60–70 days the hatchlings make their way to the sea after dark, leaving a trail of V-shaped tracks (*see* opposite).

COMMENTS This is the world's largest turtle and can weigh as much as 727 kg (1,600 lb).

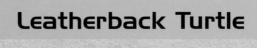

Nesting Turtles

Sea turtles live in the sea and come to land only to lay eggs. Every couple of years, the turtles travel to their breeding area and mate. The female then drags herself up onto the beach, uses her flippers to dig a pit, lays her eggs, and covers them with sand. When the young hatch, they must make their own way to the sea. Many are caught by birds and other predators.

▲ *Freshwater turtles make their nests in sandy soil near water. The broken eggshells around the entrance to this nest show it has been raided, perhaps by a fox or a raccoon.*

Barn Owl

SIZE Body and tail: up to 40 cm
(16 in); wingspan: 1.2 m (4 ft)
RANGE North and South America,
Europe, Africa, Southeast Asia, Australia
HABITAT Open areas including grassland,
desert, farmland
FOOD Small mammals such as mice and shrews
TRACKS AND SIGNS You may hear the Barn Owl's
screaming or hissing calls. Look for its pellets, too.
Owls, like other birds, bring up pellets that
contain the fur and bones they cannot digest.
Barn Owl pellets are sausage-shaped
and grey in colour. You may find
owl tracks on soft ground. They
are up to 7.5 cm (3 in) long and
the fourth toe may be turned
backwards to help it grip prey.
COMMENTS During the day
Barn Owls roost in caves, tree
hollows, or farm buildings.

Raptor Eggs

The Barn Owl lays 4–7 white eggs, about 4 cm
(1½ in) long. The Osprey lays 2–4 eggs about
6 cm (2¼ in) long, which are creamy or
pale yellow with brownish speckles. The
Peregrine Falcon lays 3 or 4 eggs about
5 cm (2 in) long. They are brown with
darker markings.

▼ *This pellet is from a wild Harpy Eagle chick in the
Amazon rainforest. It has been pulled apart to reveal that it
contains undigested claws and fur from a two-toed sloth.*

Bird Pellets

Bird pellets are easier to identify than their droppings. The pellet's contents are of great interest to the tracker. A bird cannot chew and so just gulps down certain parts of its prey, whether it can digest them or not. The indigestible parts are coughed up once or twice a day in the form of a neat pellet. Pellets are clearly different from mammal scats: they contain easily identifiable things, such as fur, feathers, bone, insect wings, and shells; and they do not smell anything like as bad!

What pellets can tell us

Pellets are valuable clues to bird activity. A pellet on the ground is a sign that a bird is nesting, roosting, or feeding nearby. If you find one, you can examine it to see what it contains and perhaps work out which species produced it. First, note where you found the pellet and sketch or

photograph it. Next, wearing disposable gloves, place the pellet on a surface, such as a plastic tray, and gently pull it apart using tweezers. If it is hard, soak it in water first.

▲ *The pellets of the Rook, a type of crow, contain much plant matter. Look for crow pellets where they forage or near their colonies.*

Which birds produce pellets?

All birds of prey bring up pellets. Owls, particularly, tend to swallow their prey almost whole. Seabirds also tend to swallow indigestible material such as fish bones and shellfish shells. Other pellet producers include storks, herons, kingfishers, crows, and waders. Even songbirds sometimes bring up pellets containing indigestible seeds or pips.

Types of pellet

OWLS Owl pellets are usually grey and, in some owls, are long and sausage-shaped. They may contain fur, feathers, insect bits, such as beetle wing cases, and bones.

OTHER BIRDS OF PREY Pellets of these birds rarely contain bone as they can usually digest the bones of their prey. They also tend to tear their prey into smaller pieces before eating. Their pellets contain fur, feathers, insect parts, beaks, and claws. Sparrowhawk pellets are up to 4 cm (1½ in) long and contain lots of feathers, while buzzard pellets are generally made up of rodent fur.

CROW FAMILY Crow pellets tend to be egg-shaped and contain lots of plant material and insect parts. There are often stones in crow pellets. Crow pellets are generally about 4.5 cm (2 in) long, while those of Rooks and jackdaws are smaller.

GULLS These may be long or round and contain fish bones, shells, and sometimes plant remains such as fruit pits. Gulls often swallow litter, such as bits of plastic, rubber bands, and string, which turns up in their pellets.

STORKS AND HERONS Storks can digest bone, but their pellets often contain fur, feathers, and insect parts. Heron pellets vary greatly, but are often oval-shaped and may contain fur from prey such as moles and voles.

▶ *This owl pellet contains pieces of bone. Unlike some other birds of prey, owls cannot digest bone.*

Identify the Bird

These pellets come from a range of birds: a buzzard, a heron and a stork, two gulls, a crow, a Rook and a jackdaw, an owl, and a sparrowhawk. See if you can guess which pellet comes from which bird.

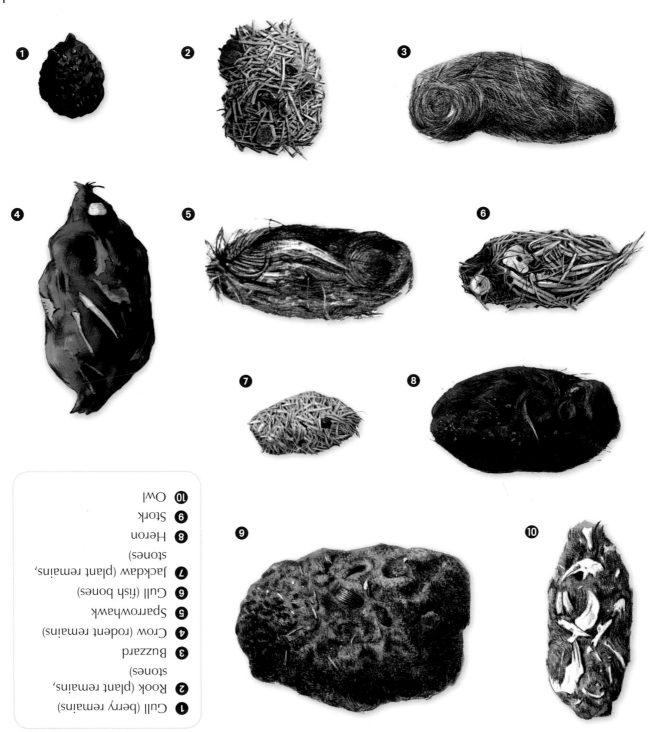

10 Owl
9 Stork
8 Heron
7 Jackdaw (plant remains, stones)
6 Gull (fish bones)
5 Sparrowhawk
4 Crow (rodent remains)
3 Buzzard
2 Rook (plant remains, stones)
1 Gull (berry remains)

▲ *A Eurasian Oystercatcher has laid its speckled eggs in this simple nest made of twigs on Skomer Island in Wales.*

Waders

Wading birds, such as sandpipers, plovers, and oystercatchers, spend much of their time on coasts or the shores of rivers and lakes, so it is quite common to see their tracks on sand or mud. They usually feed on the ground and have beaks of various lengths and shapes for probing for food to different depths. You may see the holes left by their beaks as they search for small creatures to eat. They are strong fliers, and most are also fast runners.

American Golden Plover

SIZE Body and tail: up to 28 cm (11 in); wingspan: 57 cm (22 in)
RANGE Breeds northern North America; winters South America
HABITAT Tundra, marshes, shorelines, beaches
FOOD Insects, other small creatures, berries, seeds
TRACKS AND SIGNS Look for tracks about 2.5 cm (1 in) long left by plovers as they walk along sandy beaches or muddy shores searching for food. Plovers make a shallow dip on the ground for their nest, lining it with moss and grass.
COMMENTS This bird makes amazing migration journeys of thousands of kilometres. It breeds during summer in the far north on the tundra, then flies 12,800 km (8,000 miles) south to warmer regions, where it spends the winter months.

Common Redshank

SIZE Body and tail: up to 28 cm (11 in); wingspan: 62 cm (24 in)
RANGE Europe, Asia, Africa
HABITAT Moorland, marshes, estuaries, shores
FOOD Insects, worms, and other small creatures
TRACKS AND SIGNS This is a common bird on shores and in wetland areas, such as marshes and estuaries. Watch for its bright red legs and listen for its very loud, high, whistling call. It nests on the ground in a hollow lined with plants and hidden by tall grasses. Its tracks are about 3 cm (1¼ in) long and sometimes show the back toe.
COMMENTS The Common Redshank feeds with other wading birds and is usually the first to fly off, calling noisily, if disturbed. Its call alerts other birds to possible danger.

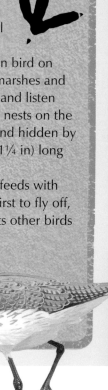

Flamingo Feeding Signs

These feeding signs were made in a marsh in the Camargue, France, by the Greater Flamingo. This wader uses filter feeding to obtain its food, treading mud in a circular motion to force small invertebrates out of the mud into the water. It then uses its beak to sieve through the water and scoop up the small creatures. At low tide, these circular imprints remain.

Eurasian Oystercatcher

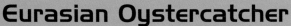

SIZE Body and tail: up to 46 cm (18 in); wingspan: 80 cm (32 in)
RANGE Europe, Asia, Africa
HABITAT Sea coasts, lakes, rivers, estuaries, beaches, fields
FOOD Mussels, cockles, worms, other small creatures
TRACKS AND SIGNS This oystercatcher species is common and often moves in large flocks, so it should be easy to spot. Like other oystercatchers, this bird has conspicuous black and white plumage and a long red beak. Its nest is a hole in the ground often lined with grass or moss. The tracks are up to 4.5 cm (1¾ in) long.
COMMENTS Oystercatchers use their long beak to prise shellfish such as cockles and mussels off rocks and to open them. Oystercatchers also probe down into mud to catch worms.

Wader Eggs

Plovers usually lay 4 eggs, which are creamy or yellowish in colour and marked with brown spots and blotches. They are about 5 cm (2 in) long. The Common Redshank lays 3–5 light brown eggs with darker speckles, which are slightly smaller than plover eggs. Oystercatchers lay 2–4 eggs, usually 3, which are creamy to light brown with darker, brownish-black markings. They are about 5.5 cm (2¼ in) long.

◄ *This nest, a deep cup of interwoven twigs, belongs to a Red-winged Blackbird, a very common bird in North America. It builds its nest either in a shrub or attached to sturdy stems, often above water.*

American Robin

SIZE Body and tail: up to 28 cm (11 in); wingspan: 40 cm (16 in)

RANGE North America, Mexico

HABITAT Forest, woodland, parks, gardens; often seen in towns and suburban areas

FOOD Worms and other small creatures, as well as fruit

TRACKS AND SIGNS You will often see this bird scurrying around searching for earthworms and then pulling them up out of the ground with a sharp tug. The nest is usually in a tree and made of grass, twigs, and mud. The robin's tracks are about 4 cm (1½ in) long. Listen for this bird's musical, whistling call and also a sharp "chup chup" sound.

COMMENTS This is a very common garden bird that is happy to live near humans. The male's bright red breast makes him easy to spot. The female's plumage is duller and paler.

Songbird Eggs

The Blackbird usually lays about 4–5 eggs, which are about 3 cm (1¼ in) long and coloured light blue with mottled, sometimes reddish-brown markings. European Starlings usually lay 5–7 eggs, which are blue or greenish-white and are just over 2.5 cm (1 in) long. The American Robin lays 2–5 light blue eggs, which are also just over 2.5 cm (1 in) long.

Seabirds

Seabirds are some of the most powerful fliers of all birds, and many travel long distances over the ocean as they search for food. Some spend nearly all their time in the air, only coming to land to mate, lay eggs, and rear their young. Seabirds are very good swimmers, and some can also dive. Their feathers form a dense, waterproof cover to protect them from cold and wet. You can see and hear squawking gulls in cities and built-up areas where they scavenge for food. Look for seabird tracks on sandy beaches and muddy shores.

▲ Like many seabirds, these Peruvian Boobies nest on cliffs, where their white droppings are highly visible.

Herring Gull

SIZE Body and tail: up to 66 cm (26 in); wingspan: 1.4 m (4½ ft)
RANGE North America, Europe, northern Asia
HABITAT Coasts, estuaries, mudflats, also urban areas
FOOD Fish, shellfish, insects, birds, eggs; also takes food from rubbish bins and dumps
TRACKS AND SIGNS You will see these large birds in any coastal areas, including cities, and hear their loud, chuckling calls. Very bold, they will scavenge around picnic sites, restaurants, and cafés. Do not get too close as they have big, sharp beaks. The nest is a simple scrape on the ground or a cliff ledge. The tracks are around 5 cm (2 in) long. Gull pellets (see pages 142–143) are a common sign.
COMMENTS Young Herring Gulls are dark brown. They do not have adult plumage until they are three years old.

Brown Pelican

SIZE Body and tail: up to 4½ ft (1.3 m); wingspan 6½ ft (2 m)
RANGE USA, Caribbean, South America
HABITAT Coasts and estuaries
FOOD Fish and other sea creatures
TRACKS AND SIGNS This pelican is easy to identify. It is the only pelican with brown feathers and the only one that dives from the air into the water to catch its food. Look for its spectacular plunges with wings held back and neck curved into an S-shape. It nests in colonies. The nest is made of sticks and built in low trees or on the ground. Its track is about 15 cm (6 in) long and shows four clawed toes.
COMMENTS If you see a Brown Pelican standing still, it might be incubating its eggs. Brown Pelicans do not sit on their eggs to keep them warm, like most birds do. Instead, they warm them using their webbed feet.

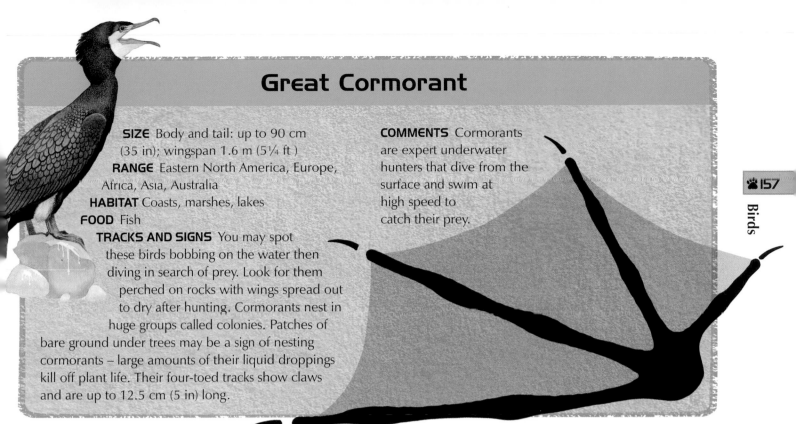

Great Cormorant

SIZE Body and tail: up to 90 cm (35 in); wingspan 1.6 m (5¼ ft)

RANGE Eastern North America, Europe, Africa, Asia, Australia

HABITAT Coasts, marshes, lakes

FOOD Fish

TRACKS AND SIGNS You may spot these birds bobbing on the water then diving in search of prey. Look for them perched on rocks with wings spread out to dry after hunting. Cormorants nest in huge groups called colonies. Patches of bare ground under trees may be a sign of nesting cormorants – large amounts of their liquid droppings kill off plant life. Their four-toed tracks show claws and are up to 12.5 cm (5 in) long.

COMMENTS Cormorants are expert underwater hunters that dive from the surface and swim at high speed to catch their prey.

Seabird Eggs

The Herring Gull lays 1–3 pale olive green or brownish eggs with dark brown speckles. The eggs are about 7 cm (2¾ in) long. Cormorant eggs are pale bluish-green with a rough, chalky white covering. The Great Cormorant usually lays 3–5 eggs, which are 6.5 cm (2½ in) long. The Brown Pelican lays a clutch of about 3 large white eggs, 7.5 cm (3 in) long.

◀ *A Herring Gull watches over its clutch of three eggs. Gulls make simple nests like this on the ground, on cliffs, and on buildings.*

Hermit Crab

If you spot what seems to be a snail or periwinkle moving surprising quickly across a beach or rock pool, you may have found a hermit crab. The hermit crab does not have a hard shell to protect its soft body, so it takes the discarded shell of another creature, such as a snail. The crab lives inside the shell and reaches out with its sharp pincers to grab food. Sea anemones often live on a hermit crab's shell, feeding on the crab's leftovers and scaring off predators.

▶ *This hermit crab has found an empty shell to protect it from predators.*

Woodlouse

SIZE Body: up to 1 cm (½ in) long
RANGE Worldwide
HABITAT Damp dark places, such as under stones and crevices in walls
FOOD Rotting plants and fungi
SIGNS Lift up a plant pot or stone in any garden or park, or a rotting branch in a wood, and you will probably see woodlice scurrying around.
COMMENTS A woodlouse has seven pairs of legs. As it grows, it has to shed the skeleton or shell on the outside of its body and grow a new one. It sheds its shell in two parts – first the back half, then the front.

Earthworm

SIZE Body: up to 30 cm (12 in) long; there are also much larger giant earthworms in Africa and Australia
RANGE Worldwide
HABITAT Surface layers of soil in fields, woods, and yards
FOOD Dead leaves and other plant materials, as well as soil
SIGNS Look for worms after heavy rain, when they may crawl to the soil surface. Keep an eye out, too, for worm "casts" on the ground. These are little worm-shaped piles of soil and plant material that have passed through the worm's body and been excreted. The worm's activity is good for soil, breaking it up and helping to get air and water into it. You may also see the earthworm's tracks, like a line in the soil.
COMMENTS Many birds love eating worms and are skilled at finding them. A blackbird on a field or garden will walk over the grass then suddenly plunge its beak into the earth and pull up a worm.

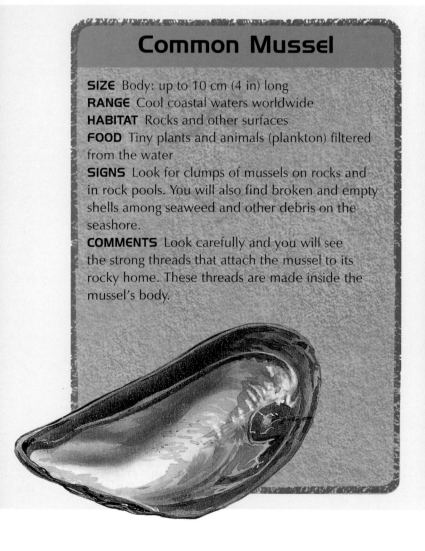

▲ *At low tide, look for tide pools like this one, filled with sea creatures such as mussels, barnacles, and starfish.*

Molluscs

Slugs and snails are some of the most familiar land-living molluscs, but the greatest range is found in the sea and on seashores. These include creatures such as mussels, limpets, periwinkles, and clams. In most molluscs the body is divided into three parts – the head, which contains the mouth and sense organs, the body, and the foot, a fleshy part of the body on which the animal moves along. Most, but not all, molluscs have a tough shell that protects the soft body. Look for mollusc shells washed up on the seashore.

Common Mussel

SIZE Body: up to 10 cm (4 in) long
RANGE Cool coastal waters worldwide
HABITAT Rocks and other surfaces
FOOD Tiny plants and animals (plankton) filtered from the water
SIGNS Look for clumps of mussels on rocks and in rock pools. You will also find broken and empty shells among seaweed and other debris on the seashore.
COMMENTS Look carefully and you will see the strong threads that attach the mussel to its rocky home. These threads are made inside the mussel's body.

Scallop

SIZE Body: up to 10 cm (4 in) long
RANGE Atlantic and Pacific oceans
HABITAT Sandy and gravel-bottomed coastal waters down to about 300 m (1,000 ft) deep
FOOD Tiny plants and animals (plankton) filtered from the water
SIGNS Look for the almost circular shells washed up on seashores.
COMMENTS A scallop swims by clapping its shells together, forcing out jets of water that push it forwards.

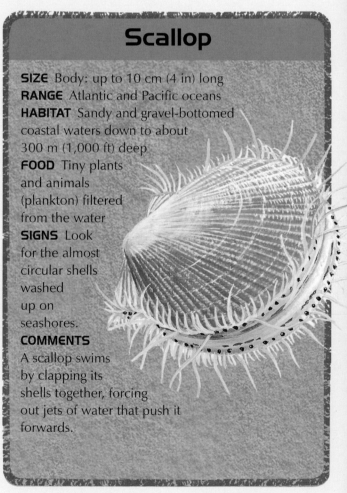

▶ *Apple snails live in water and use gills to breathe. They also have lungs for breathing in air when they come on to land to lay eggs on plant stems and when food is scarce in the water.*

Slugs

Slugs are molluscs like snails, but they do not have external shells. Like snails, slugs make slimy mucus in their body, which helps them glide over the ground. Look for the slug's glistening silvery trails. Slugs eat large amounts of leaves and other plant material and some species can be a nuisance to gardeners.

Razor Clam

SIZE Body: up to 25 cm (10 in) long
RANGE Atlantic and Pacific coasts
HABITAT Sandy-bottomed shallow water
FOOD Tiny plants and animals (plankton), which the clam filters from the water
SIGNS Razor clams live in burrows on sandy shores below the low-tide line. Look for the holes in the sand that may be a sign of a razor clam's burrow. Some razor clam burrows are just little dips in the sand, but others have raised sides. If you dig very quickly, you might uncover a clam, but clams can dig quickly too. They sometimes squirt water or sand out of the hole, so watch out!
COMMENTS This clam's long, razor-shaped shell is often washed up on seashores.

Garden Snail

SIZE Body: up to 9 cm (3½ in) long
RANGE Europe (similar species in North America and elsewhere)
HABITAT Farmland, fields, gardens – anywhere with plant life
FOOD Leaves and fruit, but will also eat dead insects and other small creatures
TRACKS AND SIGNS Look for the snail's slimy trail. It produces mucus in its body to help it move along the ground more easily and protect itself against rough surfaces. The evening and after rain are good times to look for signs of snail activity.
COMMENTS Most snails spend the day inside their shell and come out at night to find food. Lots of birds like to eat snails, and you often find empty shells.

The ant lion's trap

The ant lion is not an ant at all, but a relative of lacewings and alderflies. The adult looks rather like a dragonfly, but the larva is wingless, with large, spiny jaws. The larva digs a pit in sandy soil to catch prey, waiting in a tiny hole at the bottom for passing insects to enter the pit. Once on the pit's slopes, the prey slips and slides downwards. When it reaches the bottom, the ant lion pierces its prey with sharp, hollow jaws and sucks the juices out of its victim. Ant lions are found worldwide, most often in dry and sandy places.

Ants' nest

One of the easiest insect nests is to find is the mound-like home of the red wood ant. It is several feet high and is often made in a woodland around a tree stump, which helps to support it. Inside is a network of passages and chambers for eggs and larvae, which usually extends underground as well as into the mound itself. Twigs, grass, and pine needles cover the mound, and you may notice trails of ants coming and going from the nest.

Potter wasp

Potter wasps, or mud daubers, live alone, not in large colonies. The female builds a pot-shaped nest of mud and water on the ground or on a wall or branch. Inside there may be a number of cells. She places an egg in each cell and adds food such as caterpillars or other larvae, which she has stung and paralyzed. The chamber is then sealed. When the wasp larva hatches, it eats the food left for it, then breaks out of the chamber.

▲ *A female potter wasp makes her mud nest in the Arabian Desert.*

▲ *The ant lion larva awaits its victims in a small hole at the bottom of a pit a few inches across. Look for the pits in dry, sunny, sheltered spots, particularly on south-facing slopes.*

Cockroaches and Beetles

Most cockroaches live outside, but the kinds that live in buildings are the best known. Earwigs can be found in every garden. Beetles are one of the largest groups of insects – there are more than a quarter of a million species known. They have strong mouthparts for chewing their food and two pairs of wings. The front pair are hard and act as covers for the more delicate back wings.

▲ *Bark beetles have dug out "galleries" of holes in the bark of this tree. Each hole contains a beetle egg.*

Common Earwig

SIZE Body: up to 2 cm (¾ in) long
RANGE Europe and North America
HABITAT Damp, dark places among grass, trees, and even inside buildings
FOOD Leaves, fruit, and flowers; also eats mites and insect larvae
TRACKS AND SIGNS These are some of the easiest insects to find. Lift a stone, plant pot, or log in a damp corner, and you are likely to see earwigs scurrying away.
COMMENTS The female earwig lays her eggs in a burrow and stays with them until a few days after they hatch.

European Stag Beetle

SIZE Body: up to 8 cm (3 in) long, but many other stag beetle species are smaller
RANGE Europe; many other species worldwide
HABITAT Woodland, especially in tropical areas
FOOD Adults eat tree sap and leaves; larvae feed on the juices of rotting wood
TRACKS AND SIGNS These insects, like their cousin the Giant Stag Beetle of North America, are easy to recognize because of their large size and the huge branching jaws of the male. You are most likely to spot them in the breeding season, when rival males battle each other to win females. A good place to look is anywhere there is dead or rotting wood.
COMMENTS If a stag beetle lands on its back during a fight, it is very difficult for it to right itself again and it may get snapped up by a bird or other predator.

Diving Beetle

SIZE Body: up to 4 cm (1½ in) long

RANGE Many species worldwide

HABITAT Ponds, rivers, streams

FOOD Insect larvae, tadpoles, small fish

TRACKS AND SIGNS Look for these large beetles in ponds, using their back legs like oars to move through the water. You may see the larvae, too, which are fierce hunters. The pupae of these beetles are found in mud near the water.

COMMENTS You sometimes see these beetles flying out of the water at night. They are attracted to lights.

Stag Beetle Life Cycle

Female stag beetles usually lay their eggs in cracks in logs or dead tree stumps. The eggs hatch into worm-like larvae called grubs. As a larva feeds and grows, it sheds its skin several times and grows a new one. When the larva is fully grown, it becomes a pupa. Inside its case, the pupa does not feed while it changes into the adult form.

German Cockroach

SIZE Body: up to 2.5 cm (1 in) long

RANGE Now worldwide

HABITAT Houses, factories, restaurants

FOOD Anything eaten by people or other animals

TRACKS AND SIGNS These cockroaches leave a number of signs of their presence. Among them are little brown droppings, about the size of coffee grounds, and skins shed by young cockroaches as they grow. You may also find the little handbag-shaped containers in which the female cockroach lays her eggs. She leaves this egg case in a dark safe place before the eggs hatch.

COMMENTS Cockroaches usually hide during the day and come out at night to find food.

▼ In very soft terrain, such as sand, beetles may leave tracks with their six legs. The tracks are quite similar from species to species, apart from their size.

▲ This female American Cockroach is carrying an egg case – the square-shaped object on the right – on her abdomen.

Acknowledgments

The Publisher would like to thank the following for their kind permission to reproduce their images.

KEY
FLPA= Frank Lane Picture Agency
FLPA/HS = Frank Lane Picture Agency/Holt Studios
FLPA/MP = Frank Lane Picture Agency/Minden Pictures
MC = Magickcanoe.com (http://magickcanoe.com/)
N/PD = Nature/PhotoDisc
NPL = Nature Picture Library
NPS = National Park Service/Department of the Interior/Washington, D.C.
PL/OSF = Photo Library/Oxford Scientific Films
USDA/NRCS = United States Department of Agriculture/Natural Resources Conservation Service
USFWS = U.S. Fish and Wildlife Service/National Image Library

t = top, **b** = bottom, **c** = centre, **r** = right, **l** = left

Front cover Chris Harvey/Ardea; **back cover** Chris Harvey/Ardea (lion track); PhotoDisc (pine cones, feather); **front flap** PhotoDisc; **back flap** PhotoDisc (acorns); Adrian Davies/NPL (scat); Danielle Jerry/USFWS (wolf track).

1 Tim Fitzharris/FLPA/MP; 2–3 Jim Brandenburg/FLPA/MP; 4–5 Heidi & Hans-Juergen Koch/FLPA/MP; 6–7 Thomas Mangelsen/FLPA/MP; 8 Tom and Pat Leeson/Ardea; 9t Martin Harvey/NHPA; 9b Roger Tidman/NHPA; 10t Dave Watts/NHPA; 10b N/PD; 12t Jim Peaco/NPS; 12bl Frank Balthis/NPS; 12br Dennis Larson/USDA/NRCS; 13 Jim Peaco/NPS; 14 Danielle Jerry/USFWS; 16–17 Renee Lynn/Corbis; 18 Chris Harvey/Ardea; 20 Tim Fitzharris/FLPA/MP; 21 John Daniels/Ardea; 22 Dave Watts/NPL; 23 Mike Lane/NHPA; 24 Bev Wigney/MC; 25 PL/OSF Daniel Cox; 26t NPL/Niall Benvie; 27 Norbert Wu/FLPA/MP; 28 Dave Watts/NPL; 29 Terry Whittaker/FLPA; 30cl Mike J Thomas/FLPA; 30tl Solvin Zankl/NPL; 32 Steve Hillebrand/USFWS; 33 FLPA/Sunset; 35t David Hosking/FLPA; 35b Andrew Cooper/NPL; 36 Martin Woike/FLPA/FotoNatura; 37 Brian Kenney/PL/OSF; 38 Hans D. Dossenbach/Ardea; 39 T. Kitchin & V. Hurst/NHPA; 40 Paul A. Souders/Corbis; 41 Wendy Dennis/FLPA; 42 Geoff Trinder/Ardea; 43tl Simon Litten/FLPA; 43br Jean Hall/FLPA/HS; 45 Igor Shpilenok/NPL; 46 ZSSD/FLPA/MP; 47 James Warwick/NHPA; 48 Chris Knights/Ardea; 49 Peter Davey/FLPA; 50 Cyril Ruopso/JH Editorial/FLPA/MP; 51 Ian Redmond/NPL; 52 Terry Whittaker/FLPA; 53 Anup Shah/NPL;

54 David Hosking/FLPA; 55t Ingo Arndt/NPL; 55 inset Ian Redmond; 56 Konrad Wothe/FLPA; 57 David Tipling/NPL; 58 Roger Tidman/FLPA; 60t Jo Suderman/NPS; 60b Richard Lake/NPS; 61l N/PD; 61 inset Jo Suderman/NPS; 61r Mike Yochim/NPS; 62 Tony Heald/NPL; 64 Frans Lanting/FLPA; 66 Gerard Lacz/FLPA; 68–69 Andrew Parkinson/NPL; 70 Philippe Clement/NPL; 72 Ariadne Van Zandbergen/FLPA; 74t J. Schmidt/NPS; 74b PL/OSF; 76 Michael Quinton/FLPA/MP; 77 Angela Hampton/FLPA; 78 Tom & Pat Leeson/Ardea; 79 Nigel J. Dennis/NHPA; 80 Richard Anthony/HS/FLPA; 81 Martin Harvey/NHPA; 82 Mike Lane/FLPA/HS; 83 Richard Du Toit/NPL; 84 Brandon D. Cole/Corbis; 85 Paul Hobson/NPL; 86 Owen Newman/PL/OSF; 87 Alan Root/PL/OSF; 88 Adrian Davies/NPL; 89 Dembinsky Photo Ass./FLPA; 90cl Laurie Campbell/NHPA; 90bl George McCarthy/Corbis; 90tr John Hawkins/FLPA; 92 Tom & Pat Leeson/Ardea; 93 Sumio Harada/FLPA/MP; 94 Jamie Harron/Corbis; 95 Stephen Dalton/NHPA; 96 Donna Dewhurst/USFWS; 98 Solvin Zankl/NPL; 99 Andrew Parkinson/NPL; 100 Simon Colmer/NPL; 101 Sunset/FLPA; 102cl Bev Wigney/MC; 102br Ed Austin/Herb Jones/NPS; 103 Rosalie La Rue/NPS; 104 Bev Wigney/MC; 105l J. Schmidt/NPS; 105r

Elliot Neep/PL/OSF; 106 Francois Savigny/NPL; 107 Staffan Widstrand/NPL; 108 Gerard Lacz/FLPA; 110 Dave Watts/NPL; 111 Joe McDonald/Corbis; 112 Don Hitchcock; 113 Dave Watts/NPL; 114 Staffan Widstrand/Corbis; 115 Dave Watts/NHPA; 116–117 Theo Allofs/Corbis; 118 David Kjaer/NPL; 119 Bev Wigney/MC; 120 Malcolm Schuyl/FLPA; 121 Christian Ziegler/FLPA/MP; 122 M. Watson/Ardea; 124t, 124b Heidi & Hans-Juergen Koch/FLPA/MP; 125t Michael & Patricia Fogden/FLPA/MP; 125b Steimer/ARCO/NPL; 126 Theo Allofs/Corbis; 127 Konrad Wothe/FLPA/MP; 128 Kennan Ward/Corbis; 129 Bev Wigney/MC; 130–131 Gary Vestal/Getty Images; 132 Mike Wilkes/NPL; 133 Philippe Clement/NPL; 134l N/PD; 134rt Greg Weiler/USFWS; 134rb N/PD; 136 Mike Jones/FLPA; 137 Niall Benvie/NPL; 138 David Hosking/FLPA; 139 Tom Vezo/NPL; 140 Dietmar Nill/NPL; 141 Pete Oxford/FLPA/MP; 142l Tony Wharton/FLPA; 142b Jeff Foott/NPS; 144 Annie Poole/Corbis; 145 Jean E. Roche/NPL; 146 Fritz Polking/FLPA; 147 Dan Guravich/Corbis; 148 Brian Lightfoot/NPL; 149t Don Smith/FLPA; 149b Tupper Ansel Blake/USFWS; 151 Simon Hosking/FLPA; 152 Christian Jansky; 154 Roger Wilmshurst/FLPA; 155 Larry Michael/NPL; 156 Jim Clare/NPL; 157 Roger Wilmshurst/FLPA; 158bl Roger Tidman/FLPA; 158–159 Dave Menke/USFWS; 159t Jim Peaco/NPS; 159c David Hosking/FLPA; 159b Donna Dewhurst/USFWS; 160–161 Ingo Arndt/NPL; 162 Gary K. Smith/FLPA; 163 N/PD; 164 Stuart Westmorland/Corbis; 165 Matthew Perry/USFWS; 166 Bev Wigney/MC; 167 Geoff du Feu/Ardea; 169bl Heidi & Hans-Juergen Koch/FLPA/MP; 169br N/PD; 170 Bev Wigney/MC; 171t Ian Rose/FLPA; 171b N/PD; 172 MPFL/PA; 173 Fritz Polking/FLPA; 174 Kim Taylor/NPL; 177t Ray Bird/FLPA; 177bl NPL/Premaphotos; 177br Jane Burton/NPL; 178 Myers/NPS; 179 Kim Taylor/NPL; 180, 181 Bev Wigney/MC; 182 MPictures/FLPA; 183 John Good/NPS; 186t Fritz Polking/FLPA; 187c Danielle Jerry/USFWS; 187b Don Hitchcock

Answers to Tracks Quiz, pages 184–185: 1 Pheasant 2 Red Deer 3 Crocodile 4 Lynx 5 Gecko 6 Otter 7 Woodpecker 8 Squirrel 9 Snapping Turtle 10 Fox 11 Tasmanian Devil 12 Beetle 13 Goose 14 Rat 15 Chimpanzee 16 Hare or rabbit 17 Emu 18 Brown Bear 19 Frog 20 Skunk